Little Bulldozer helps again

Story by Annette Smith
Illustrated by Marina McAllan

Sell your books at
sellbackyourBook.com!
Go to sellbackyourBook.com
and get an instant price quote.
We even pay the shipping - see
what your old books are worth
today!

Inspected By:Lorie_Martinez

00027290768

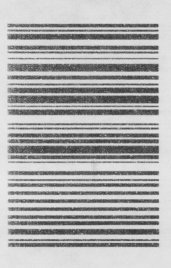

00027290768

G

"Hello, Little Bulldozer,"
said Big Bulldozer.
"I'm going down to the river
to make a road."

"Can I help?" said Little Bulldozer.

"No, not today," said Big Bulldozer.

4

Day after day, Big Truck came
to help Big Bulldozer
make the road.

"Can I help, too?"
said Little Bulldozer.

"No, not today," said Big Truck.

6

One day Big Truck shouted, "I'm going down in the mud! Help! Help! I'm stuck in the mud, down here at the river. I can't get out!"

8

Big Bulldozer said,
"I will come
and get you out."
He looked down at the mud.
"No!" he said.   "I can't!
I'm too big and heavy.
I will get
stuck in the mud, too."

9

Little Bulldozer said, "I can help.
I'm not big and heavy."

Big Bulldozer said,
"Yes, you are **little**!
Here you are. Here's a rope.
You will not sink down
into the mud like me."

Little Bulldozer went all the way down to Big Truck with the rope

He tied the rope on.

13

Big Bulldozer went back up the road with the rope. *V-room.*

And Big Truck came
up out of the mud!

16